A Scary Storm
The Story of Jesus and a Stormy Sea

We are grateful to the following team of authors for their contributions to *God Loves Me,* a Bible story program for young children. This Bible story, one of a series of fifty-two, was written by Patricia L. Nederveld, managing editor for CRC Publications. Suggestions for using this book were developed by Jesslyn DeBoer, a freelance author from Grand Rapids, Michigan. Yvonne Van Ee, an early childhood educator, served as project consultant and wrote *God Loves Me,* the program guide that accompanies this series of Bible storybooks.

Nederveld has served as a consultant to Title I early childhood programs in Colorado. She has extensive experience as a writer, teacher, and consultant for federally funded preschool, kindergarten, and early childhood programs in Colorado, Texas, Michigan, Florida, Missouri, and Washington, using the *High/Scope* Education Research Foundation curriculum. In addition to writing the *Bible Footprints* church curriculum for four- and five-year-olds, Nederveld edited the revised *Threes* curriculum and the first edition of preschool through second grade materials for the *LiFE* curriculum, all published by CRC Publications.

DeBoer has served as a church preschool leader and as coauthor of the preschool-kindergarten materials for the *LiFE* curriculum published by CRC Publications. She has also written K-6 science and health curriculum for Christian Schools International, Grand Rapids, Michigan, and inspirational gift books for Zondervan Publishing House.

Van Ee is a professor and early childhood program advisor in the Education Department at Calvin College, Grand Rapids, Michigan. She has served as curriculum author and consultant for Christian Schools International and wrote the original *Story Hour* organization manual and curriculum materials for fours and fives.

Photo on page 5: Comstock; photo on page 20: Rosanne Olson/Tony Stone Images.

Library of Congress Cataloging-in-Publication Data

Nederveld, Patricia L., 1944-
     A scary storm: the story of Jesus and a stormy sea/Patricia L. Nederveld.
        p. cm. — (God loves me; bk. 35)
     Summary: A simple retelling, in rhyming text, of the Bible story
in which Jesus saves his friends by calming the wind and sea. Includes
follow-up activities.
     ISBN 1-56212-304-1
     1. Stilling of the storm (Miracle)—Juvenile literature.
[1. Stilling of the storm (Miracle). 2. Jesus Christ—Miracles.
3. Bible stories—N.T.] I. Title. II. Series: Nederveld, Patricia L., 1944-
God loves me; bk. 35.
BT367.S74N43 1998
232.9'55—dc21   97-52272
                                               CIP
                                             AC

10 9 8 7 6 5 4 3 2 1

A Scary Storm
The Story of Jesus and a Stormy Sea

PATRICIA L. NEDERVELD

ILLUSTRATIONS BY ANGELA JARECKI

CRC Publications
Grand Rapids, Michigan

This is a story from God's book, the Bible.

It's for say name(s) of your child(ren). It's for me too!

Luke 8:22-25

So many people—so much to say!

t makes Jesus tired—he needs time away!

Jesus leaves
with his
friends—
they drift out to
sea.
The night is as
peaceful
as peaceful can
be.

The waves are
so gentle,
the moon
spreads its light.
And Jesus looks
ready
to sleep through
the night!

But up comes a storm—it rolls over the sea.

Fierce thunder and lightning—waves big as can be!

" **J**esus, wake up
and save us—
or surely we'll
die!
This storm is so
scary!"
his frightened
friends cry.

"Why are you frightened? Please trust me today." Then Jesus speaks to the winds— and the storm goes away!

16

The waves become gentle, moonbeams cover the sea.
The night feels as peaceful as peaceful can be.

B ut the men in the boat are amazed at the sight.
"The winds and the waves obeyed Jesus tonight!"

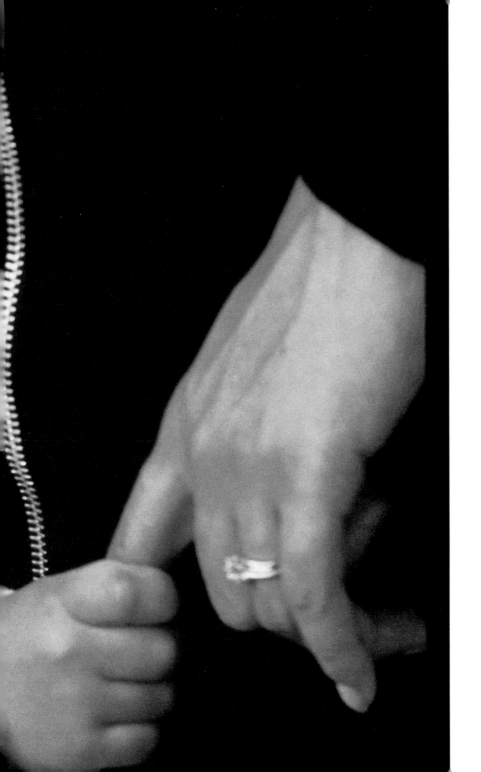

I wonder if you know that Jesus takes care of you too, even when it's stormy outside . . .

Dear Jesus, thank you that you are stronger than the scariest storm! We know you take care of us when we're frightened. Amen.

Suggestions for Follow-up

Opening

Greet your little ones with a gentle hug and whisper, "I'm so glad God takes care of you." Help children express their joy in seeing each other again.

When you gather the children around you to hear the story, ask them if they are ever scared. Allow each child to tell about a scary experience or things that frighten them. Help younger children communicate their fears by naming some things that scare them. You may want to start by telling the children about a fear you had when you were young. When everyone has had a turn, ask the children to listen very carefully to the story so they can tell you who is even stronger than a scary storm.

Learning Through Play

Learning through play is the best way! The following activity suggestions are meant to help you provide props and experiences that will invite the children to play their way into the Scripture story and its simple truth. Try to provide plenty of time for the children to choose their own activities and to play individually. Use group activities sparingly—little ones learn most comfortably with a minimum of structure.

1. Set up a water table with a baby bathtub or other shallow container, and provide toy boats for children to sail. You'll probably want to protect the floor and table with plastic or newspaper and keep a mop nearby. Old T-shirts or smocks will help keep your little ones dry.

Pose this question as they play: "I wonder what would happen if the boats were in a storm?" Perhaps the children will want to make stormy waves with their hands. You may need to remind them to be kind to others as they splash and to keep the stormy waters inside the container. Wonder with the children if they would be scared if they were in a boat during a storm. Tell them how you would feel and share your assurance that Jesus cares for you. Remind your little ones that Jesus is more powerful than a scary storm.

2. As your little ones play in the housekeeping area, invite them to imagine it is storming outside. Will they be afraid? What will they do to take care of their babies? What do they do at home when it's stormy outside? Suggest a prayer they can say when it's storming, or try singing "Jesus Loves Me" (Songs Section, *God Loves Me* program guide) louder than the thunder.

3. Ahead of time, copy the medal pattern (see Pattern N, Patterns Section, *God Loves Me* program guide) on card stock. Cut them out, and lay a supply on a table along with bright colored highlighters and small stickers or stars. Encourage the children to decorate the border and backside of the medals. Older children may enjoy adding glitter. To make a nontoxic glitter, add five drops of food coloring to ½ cup (.12 L) of salt. Shake vigorously in a covered container. Pour small amounts into salt shakers, and show the children how to rub a

glue stick around the edges or all over the medal. (You might want to cover the table with newspaper to catch the spills.) Read the words God Cares for Me aloud as you pin the medals to the children's clothing.

4. Play "Rain and Thunder" with children who like active games. Begin by reminding the children that these ways of touching each other are good: a handshake, a pat on the shoulder, a hug. Hitting and squeezing do not feel good! Then tell the children that you will chant, "It's raining, raining, raining, raining . . ." while they hop, skip, or walk around the room. When they hear you say "thunder," they should stop, find a friend, and give that person a good touch. Older children will enjoy taking turns calling the rain and thunder cues. Sign the cues for a child who is hearing impaired. Remember that some children may not feel comfortable with touching or with this level of activity and interaction. Encourage these little ones to try the game, but allow them to decide how long they want to participate.

5. Provide a stack of blankets and stuffed animals or dolls. Invite your little ones to snuggle with a favorite toy while you sing together one or more stanzas of "God Is So Good" (Songs Section, *God Loves Me* program guide). Sing the words softly like a lullaby.

> *God is so good . . .*
> *He cares for me . . .*

God keeps me safe . . .
Thank you, dear God . . .
—Stanzas 1 and 2, traditional

Closing

Gather the children around you, and join hands to form a circle. Sing the last stanza of "He's Got the Whole World" (Songs Section, *God Loves Me* program guide):

> *He's got everybody here in his hands . . .*

Substitute the names of your children for *everybody* as you sing the stanza again. Raise your joined hands in praise as you say, "Thank you, God. Amen."

At Home

What things frighten your child the most? Scary storms, barking dogs, the dark? You can help your child deal confidently with these situations. Tell your child about fears you experienced at the same age and how you handled them.

When your child is afraid, cuddle together in a favorite rocker as you sing "Jesus Loves Me." Explore scary spots in your home with a flashlight or during the day in the bright sunlight. Say this Bible verse over and over with your child: "I will trust in God. I will not be afraid" (Ps. 56:4, NIrV). Wrap yourself and your little one snugly in a blanket, and help your child imagine that God's arms are wrapped around you.

Old Testament Stories

Blue and Green and Purple Too! *The Story of God's Colorful World*

It's a Noisy Place! *The Story of the First Creatures*

Adam and Eve *The Story of the First Man and Woman*

Take Good Care of My World! *The Story of Adam and Eve in the Garden*

A Very Sad Day *The Story of Adam and Eve's Disobedience*

A Rainy, Rainy Day *The Story of Noah*

Count the Stars! *The Story of God's Promise to Abraham and Sarah*

A Girl Named Rebekah *The Story of God's Answer to Abraham*

Two Coats for Joseph *The Story of Young Joseph*

Plenty to Eat *The Story of Joseph and His Brothers*

Safe in a Basket *The Story of Baby Moses*

I'll Do It! *The Story of Moses and the Burning Bush*

Safe at Last! *The Story of Moses and the Red Sea*

What Is It? *The Story of Manna in the Desert*

A Tall Wall *The Story of Jericho*

A Baby for Hannah *The Story of an Answered Prayer*

Samuel! Samuel! *The Story of God's Call to Samuel*

Lions and Bears! *The Story of David the Shepherd Boy*

David and the Giant *The Story of David and Goliath*

A Little Jar of Oil *The Story of Elisha and the Widow*

One, Two, Three, Four, Five, Six, Seven! *The Story of Elisha and Naaman*

A Big Fish Story *The Story of Jonah*

Lions, Lions! *The Story of Daniel*

New Testament Stories

Jesus Is Born! *The Story of Christmas*

Good News! *The Story of the Shepherds*

An Amazing Star! *The Story of the Wise Men*

Waiting, Waiting, Waiting! *The Story of Simeon and Anna*

Who Is This Child? *The Story of Jesus in the Temple*

Follow Me! *The Story of Jesus and His Twelve Helpers*

The Greatest Gift *The Story of Jesus and the Woman at the Well*

A Father's Wish *The Story of Jesus and a Little Boy*

Just Believe! *The Story of Jesus and a Little Girl*

Get Up and Walk! *The Story of Jesus and a Man Who Couldn't Walk*

A Little Lunch *The Story of Jesus and a Hungry Crowd*

A Scary Storm *The Story of Jesus and a Stormy Sea*

Thank You, Jesus! *The Story of Jesus and One Thankful Man*

A Wonderful Sight! *The Story of Jesus and a Man Who Couldn't See*

A Better Thing to Do *The Story of Jesus and Mary and Martha*

A Lost Lamb *The Story of the Good Shepherd*

Come to Me! *The Story of Jesus and the Children*

Have a Great Day! *The Story of Jesus and Zacchaeus*

I Love You, Jesus! *The Story of Mary's Gift to Jesus*

Hosanna! *The Story of Palm Sunday*

The Best Day Ever! *The Story of Easter*

Goodbye—for Now *The Story of Jesus' Return to Heaven*

A Prayer for Peter *The Story of Peter in Prison*

Sad Day, Happy Day! *The Story of Peter and Dorcas*

A New Friend *The Story of Paul's Conversion*

Over the Wall *The Story of Paul's Escape in a Basket*

A Song in the Night *The Story of Paul and Silas in Prison*

A Ride in the Night *The Story of Paul's Escape on Horseback*

The Shipwreck *The Story of Paul's Rescue at Sea*

Holiday Stories

Selected stories from the New Testament to help you celebrate the Christian year

Jesus Is Born! *The Story of Christmas*

Good News! *The Story of the Shepherds*

An Amazing Star! *The Story of the Wise Men*

Hosanna! *The Story of Palm Sunday*

The Best Day Ever! *The Story of Easter*

Goodbye—for Now *The Story of Jesus' Return to Heaven*

These fifty-two books are the heart of *God Loves Me,* a Bible story program designed for young children. Individual books (or the entire set) and the accompanying program guide *God Loves Me* are available from CRC Publications (1-800-333-8300).